WHERE'S WILLY?

Have you spotted Dick?

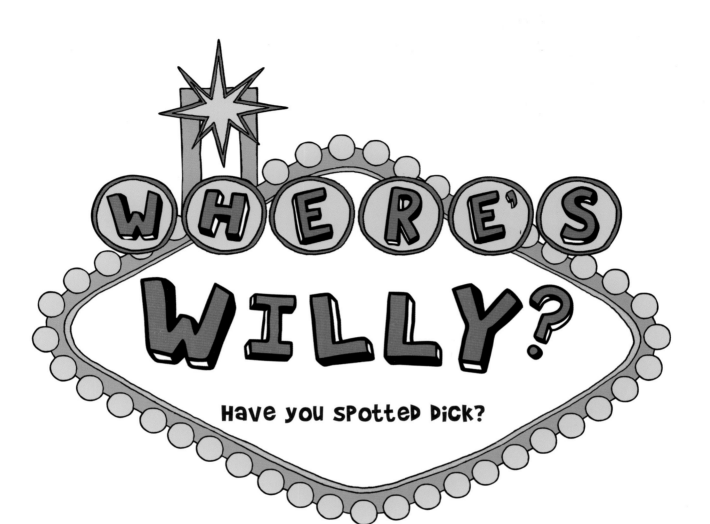

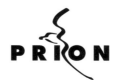

PRION

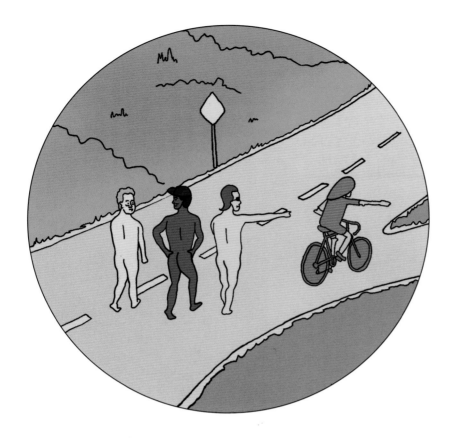

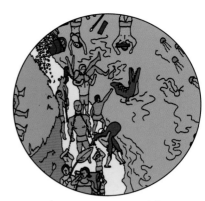

1. South Sea Schlong

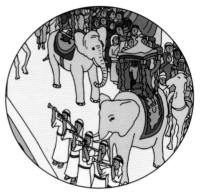

5. Persian Percy

You'll find a selection of willies on all of the spreads in this book. First of all you need to find Willy himself. He's the cheeky one dressed in purple, with purple pants and a purple helmet... you get the idea. Accompanying him on his trip around the world are his three best chums, so you'll need to look out for them too. Happy hunting!

Published in Great Britain in 2010 by Prion
an imprint of the
Carlton Publishing Group
20 Mortimer Street
London W1T 3JW

Copyright © 2010 Carlton Publishing Group

Illustrated by WINGS
The Bright Agency
www.thebrightagency.com

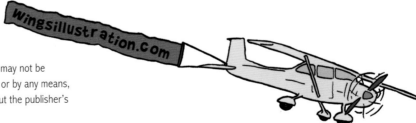

A catalogue record for this book is available from the British Library

ISBN 978-1-85375-798-3

Printed in Dubai

10 9 8 7 6 5 4 3 2

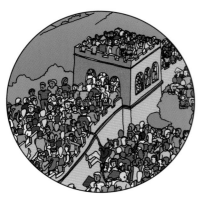

2. Great Willy of China

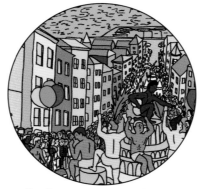

3. Sausage Festival

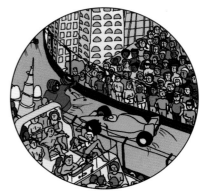

4. Tools in the fast lane

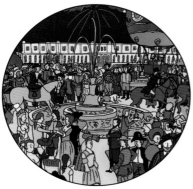

6. Members-only Ball

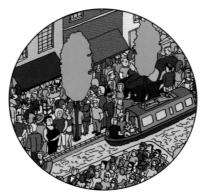

7. Seedy City

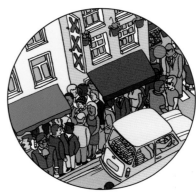

8. Private Dick Needed

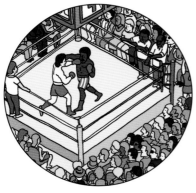

9. Ding-a-ling

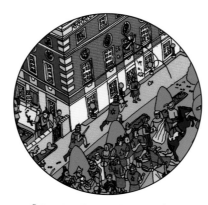

10. Once a Knight...

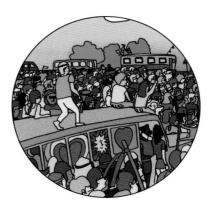

11. Summer of Love Truncheon

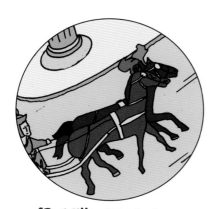

12. Willy Maximus

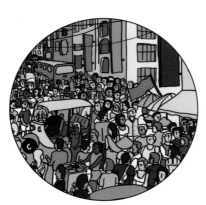

13. Bangkok not-so-Dangerous

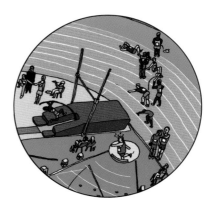

14. Sporting Lads

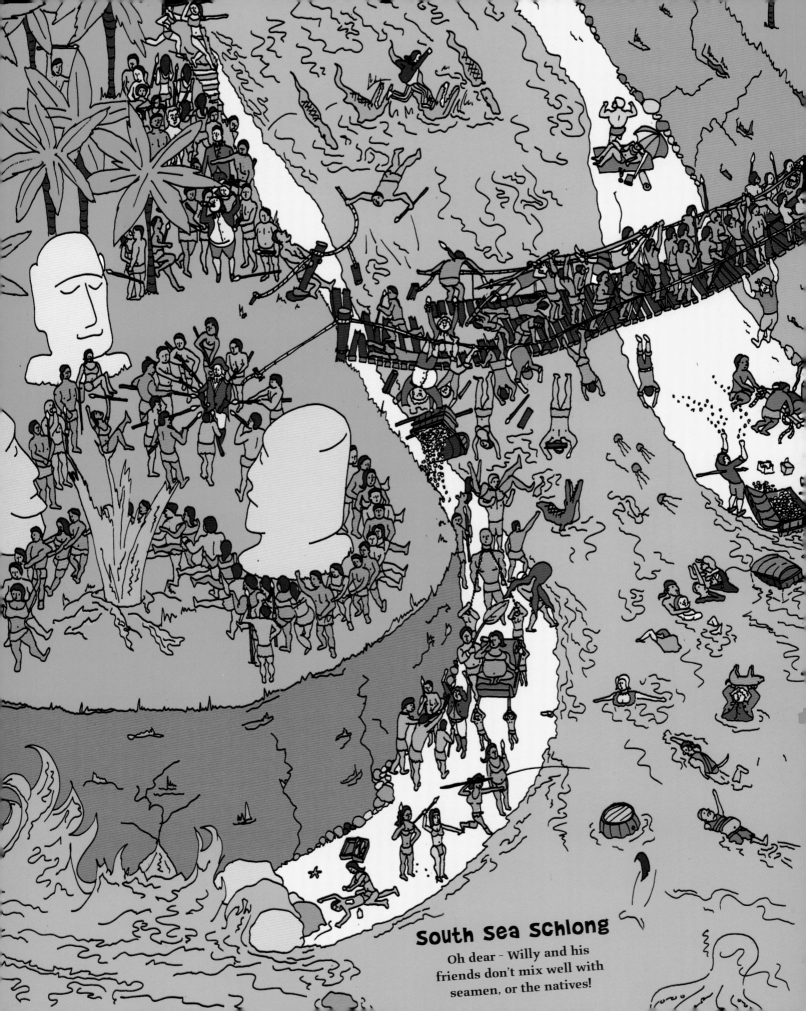

South Sea Schlong

Oh dear - Willy and his
friends don't mix well with
seamen, or the natives!

Great Willy
Of China
Is that a chopper flying through the air? I hope it doesn't throw a rod on the way down.

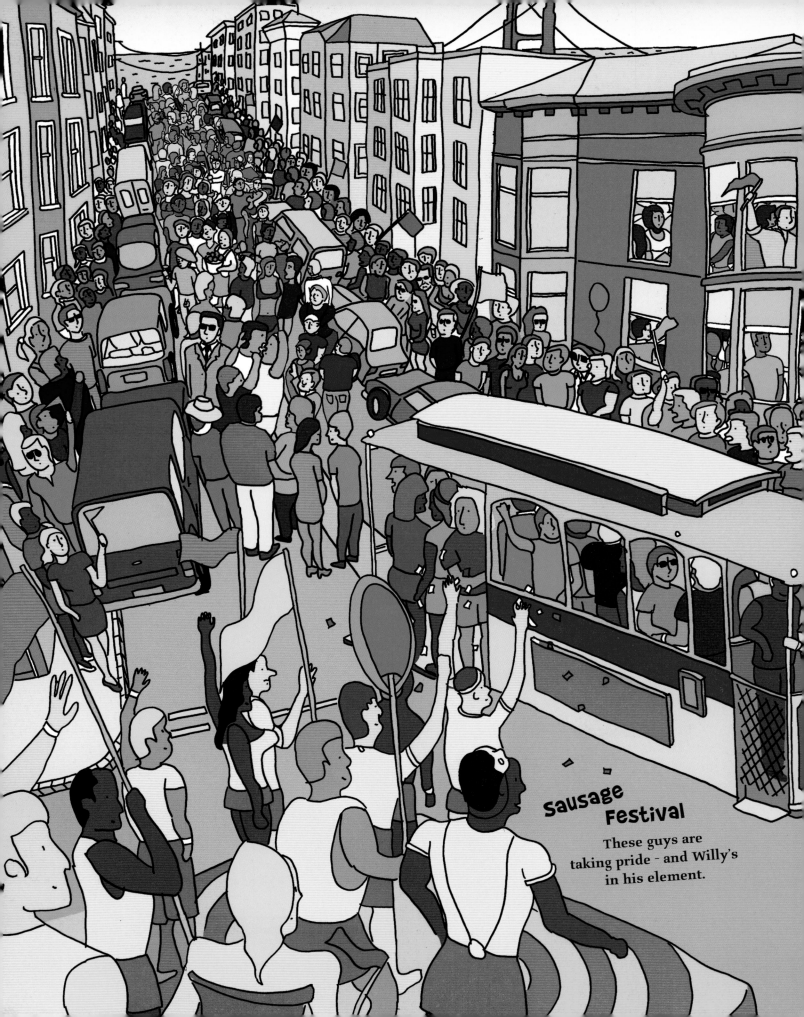

Sausage Festival

These guys are taking pride - and Willy's in his element.

Z

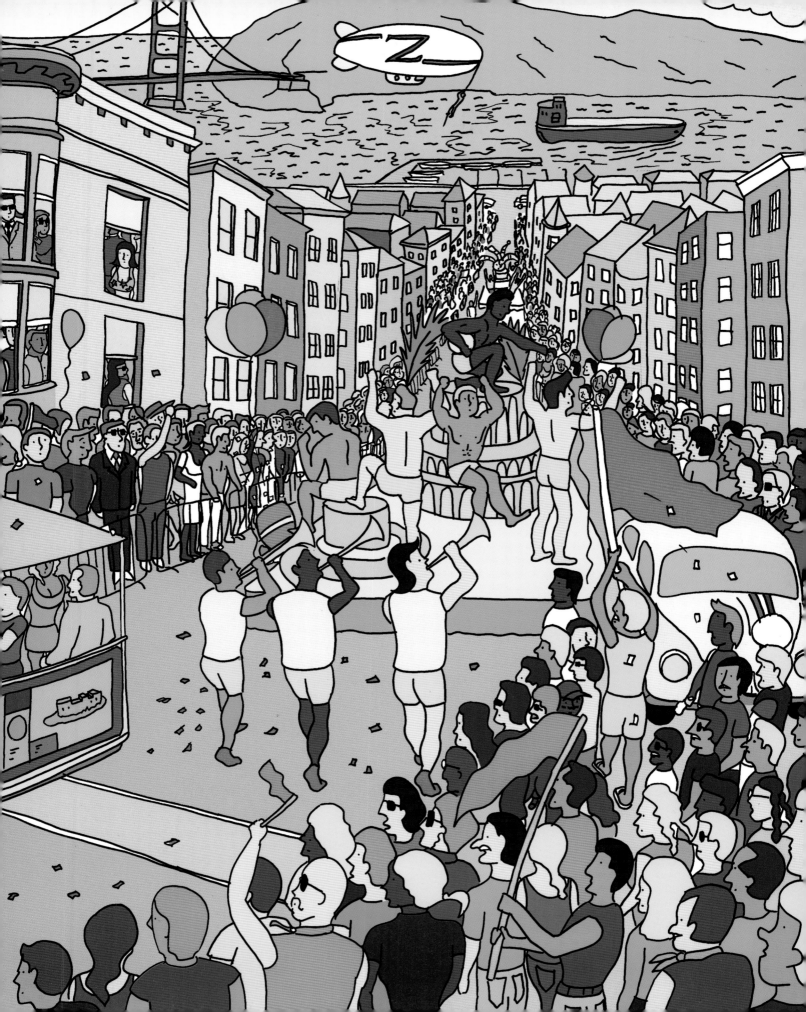

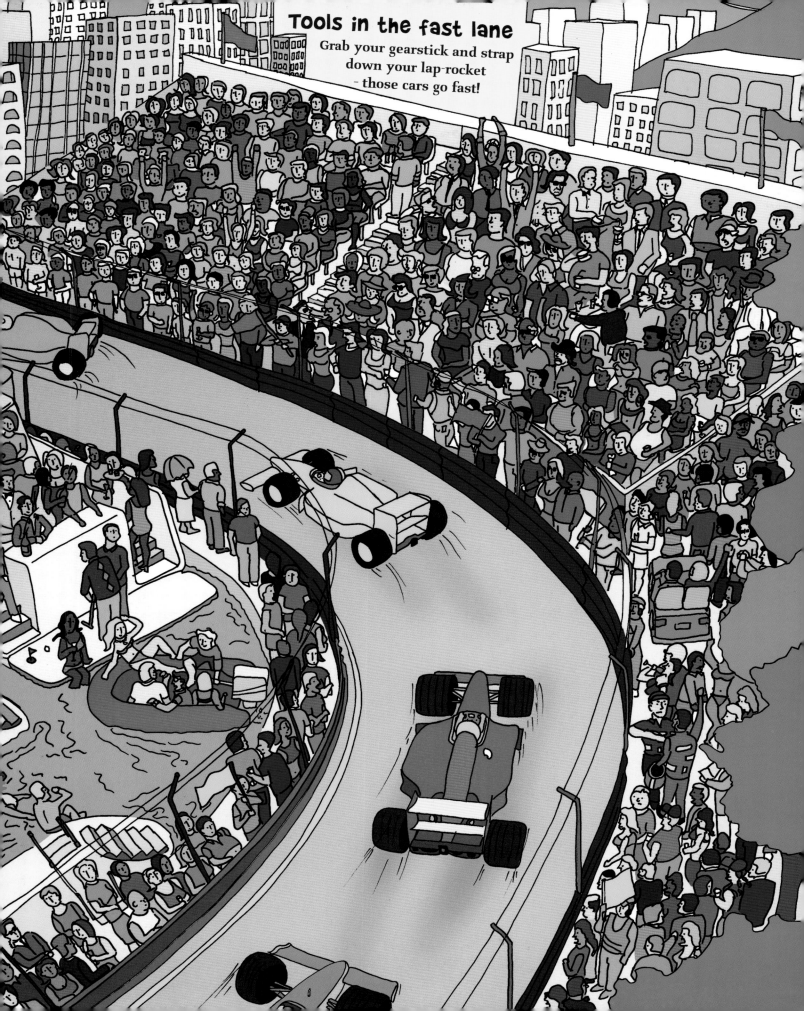

Tools in the fast lane
Grab your gearstick and strap
down your lap-rocket
- those cars go fast!

Persian Percy

There were tales from 1001 nights. Luckily you only need to find one Willy and his three chums.

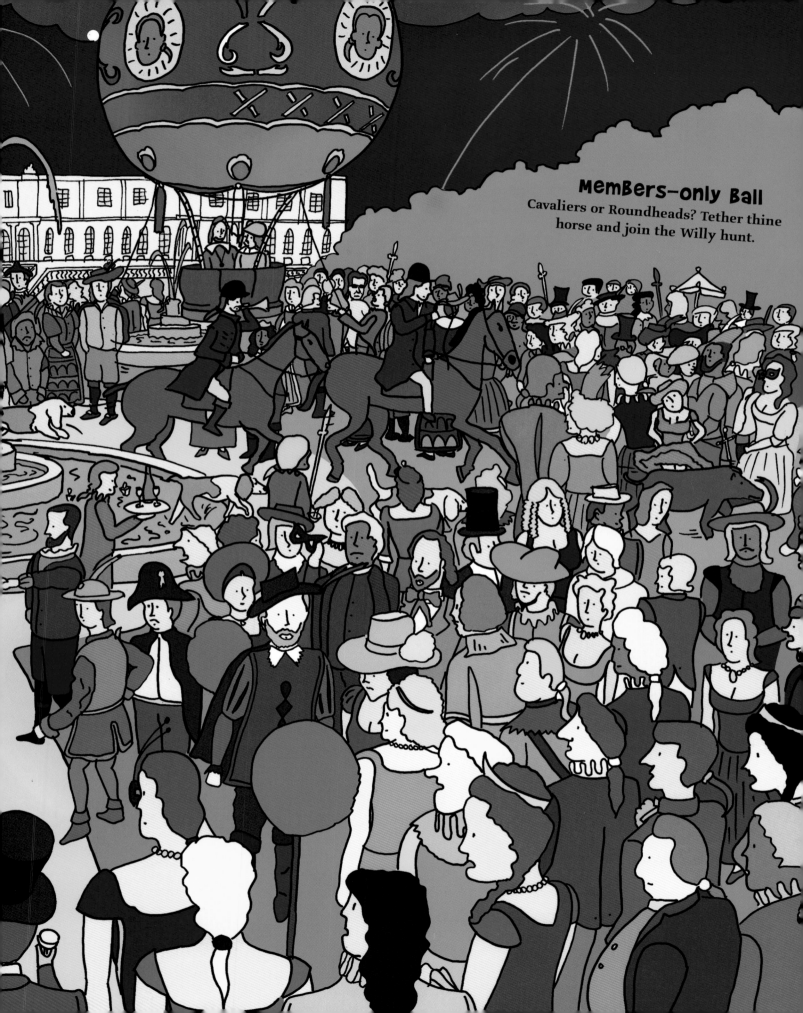

Members-only Ball
Cavaliers or Roundheads? Tether thine horse and join the Willy hunt.

Seedy City
Look at all the ladies of the night in the windows. Willy will be trying hard to find them.

BANK

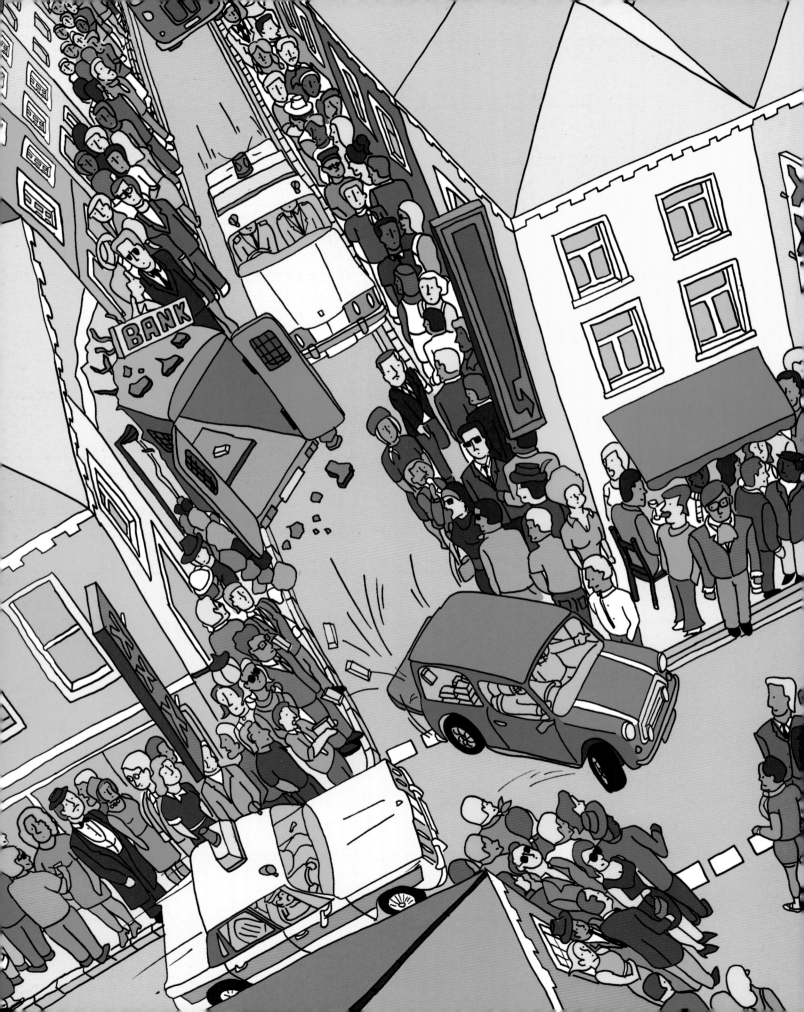

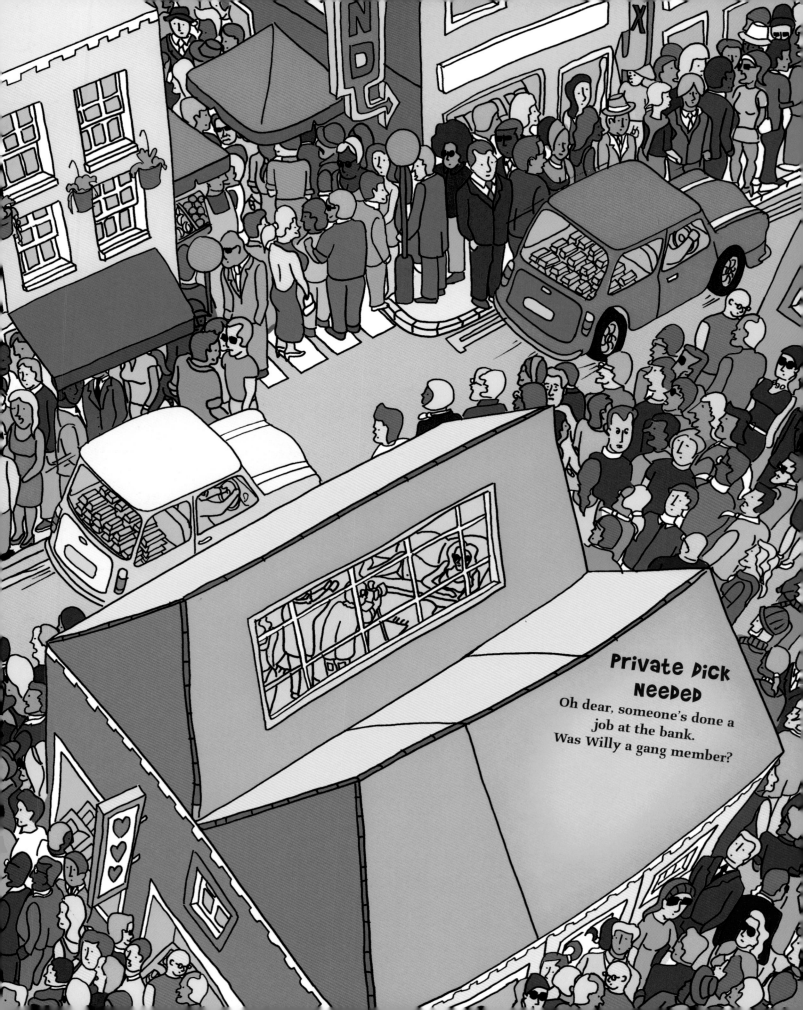

Private Dick
Needed
Oh dear, someone's done a
job at the bank.
Was Willy a gang member?

Vs
9

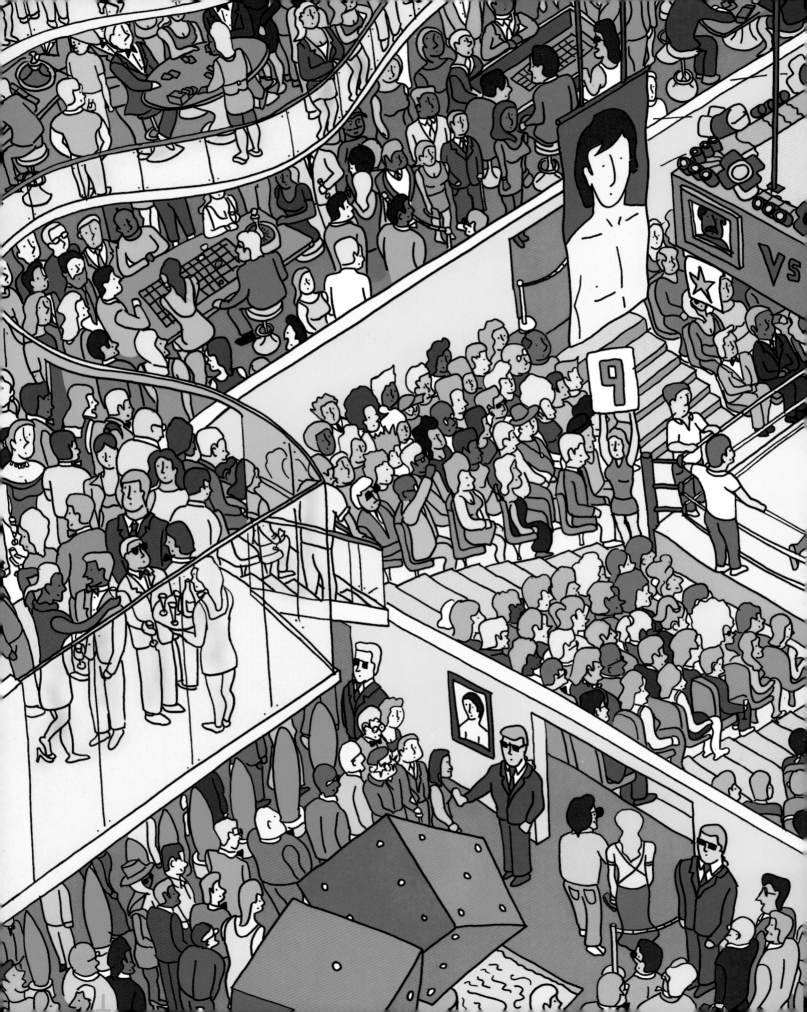

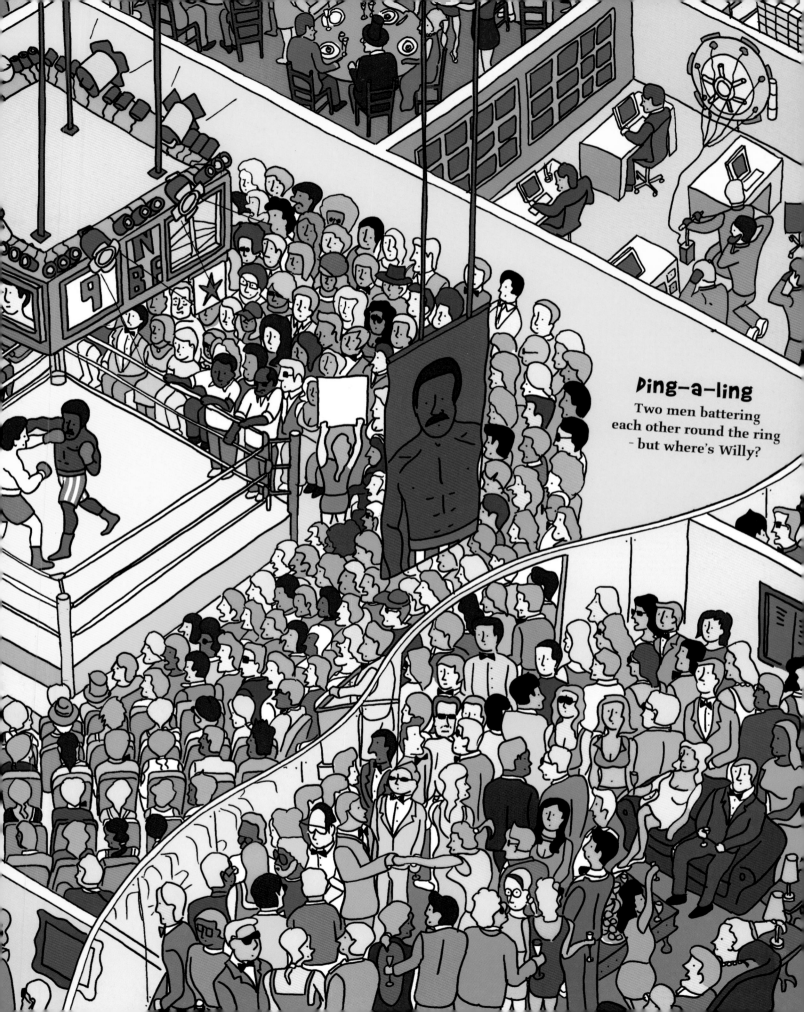

Ding-a-ling

Two men battering
each other round the ring
- but where's Willy?

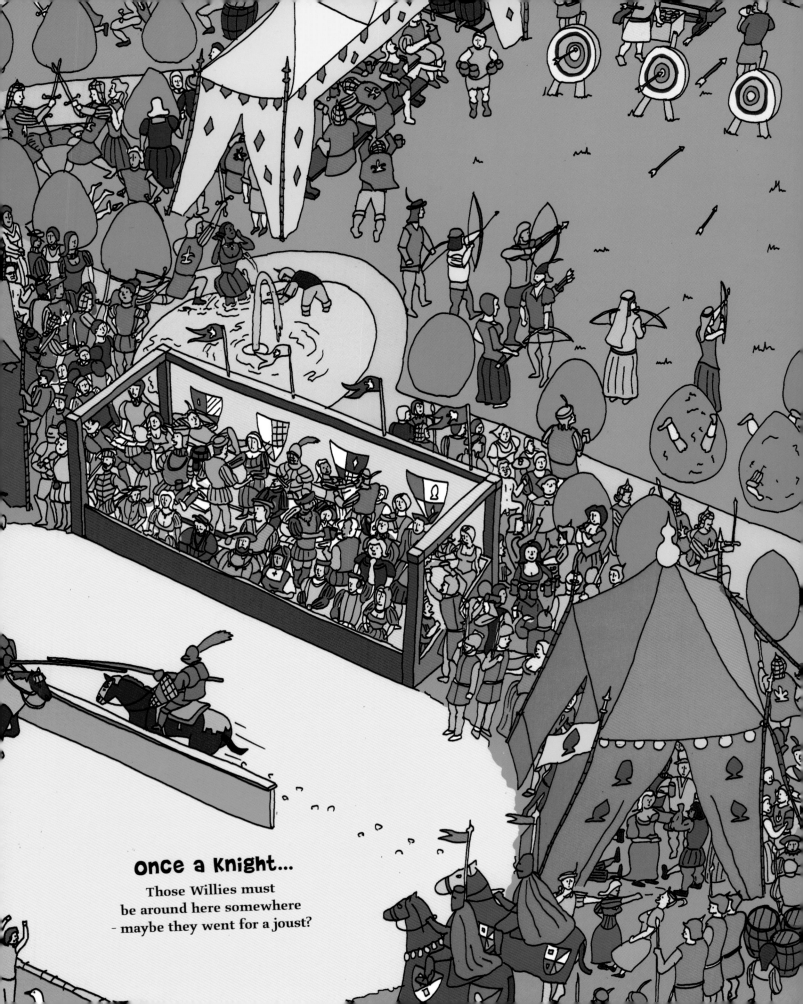

once a Knight...

Those Willies must
be around here somewhere
- maybe they went for a joust?

Summer of Love Truncheon

It's all peace & love at this groovy festival, but are Willy and his chums getting their rocks off?

Willy Maximus
Friends, Romans, countrymen – lend me your willies!

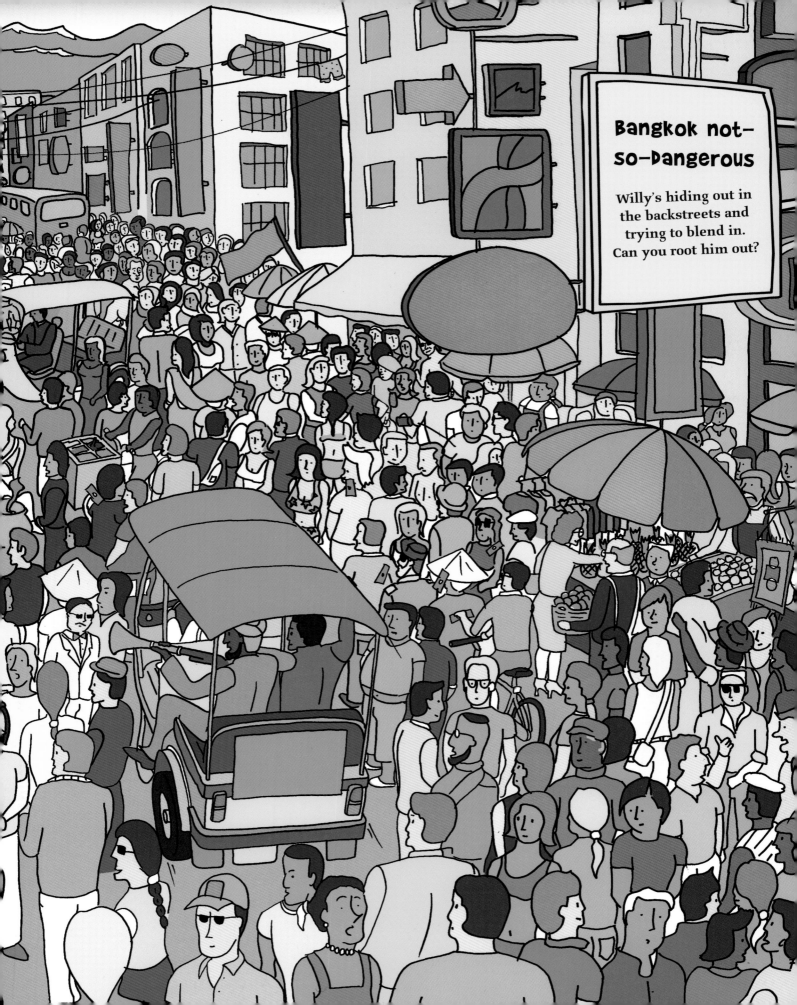

Bangkok not-so-Dangerous

Willy's hiding out in the backstreets and trying to blend in. Can you root him out?

Sporting Lads
Anyone for some javelin?
Make sure you don't
pull a love muscle.